killAR-15

How Our Culture Creates Killer 15-Year-Olds

By
Anthony Ferraioli, M.D.

Contents

FOREWORD

This was a tough book to write and it will be a tough one to read.
You'll find that it's quite blunt and to the point in places (though never meant to be rude or mean spirited); it's the book I've been wanting to write for some years but hesitated.
I finally wrote it because people need to read it---and because people have been asking me to write it.
So I've kept it short, rather sharp at times, and to the point.

The why:

When I'm asked to make a professional assessment on the news about mass shootings, I'm often stuck: do I really tell them what I know or do I hold back and give it the superficial treatment that I know will be easier to digest?
I mostly stick with the latter, in part because I get about three minutes on average to make my

comment, often about subjects that take YEARS to discuss with people who actually WANT to know and who understand what they're asking me to explain.
Talking to random people for three minutes when I'm on the news is very different.

Asking the wrong questions:

But what I want to say on the news; what I really want to get across when I'm asked about yet another kid committing a heinous act with a firearm at a school is this: it didn't start with just that kid---so stop asking me about how that particular kid could have done such a thing.

Systemic problem:

It started with the combination of our culture's skill-less parenting epidemic (more on that later), along with the steady decline of basic humanity and substance in our culture.
It didn't start with just that kid.

It started with the adults who raised that kid and with the adults who raised that kid's parents. And so on, and so on, back through the generations of trauma and skill-less parenting.

The culture piece:

And it started with our increasingly disposable and distracted culture; our increasingly aggressive, miserable, and savage culture that's devoid of real meaning and real value in favor of bottom-line profits, sales and marketing, quick fixes, various addictions (including cell-phone addiction), and self-glorification.
A culture whose industries---from healthcare to clothing, from education to food products---care only about bottom-line profits and sacrifice real quality. Nobody cares and nobody matters. People don't matter. Relationships don't matter. Products and services are disposable, fake.
And people are too.
Sell, sell, sell.
Buy, buy, buy.

Don't stop.
Don't think.
Don't reflect.
Stay numbed up.
Stay dumbed down.
Keep your head down in your cell phone. No eye contact.
Expressionless faces.
And don't forget to take a selfie and post how great you and your life are.
Smile for that.
A culture of knee-jerk reactions and no real leadership---from homes to offices, from government to corporate boardrooms.
A polarized, out-of-balance culture that uses logic without heart to fight all the time.
Pure logic fights without relationship.
No relating.
Just arguing points.
Out-logic-ing one another.

No core:

Our culture has devolved into convenience over what's actually right; we lack integrity in order to grow the bottom-line.
We lack a basic moral core.

We have no common-sense morality at all.
No loyalty.
No commitment.
No patience.
No self-sacrifice.
No leadership.
We are a short-term, "gotta get mine" culture.
Instant gratification.
We are a culture of addicts.
Selfies, porn, reality-shows, media and sports heroes, money.

Here's the point:

We burn out, just like drug addicts burn out.
And kids see and feel no real in any of this.
On some level, they know.
In their numbness, they feel it.
They have no hope.
They see no future.
They can't acknowledge and talk out loud about thoughts and feelings (fear, hopes, anger, shame, guilt, love, hate, self-hate), because nobody has the time or energy---or the knowledge or skill-set---to talk to them about anything of substance.

Logic and goals without heart:

The adults around them only have their weird language of "goals", "consequences", and "actionable items"---but are not actually alive and sentient themselves; they might try therapy, but the therapists are talking the same non-sentient language because that's all the insurance industry will let them do.
Nothing gets processed and no healing gets done.
Kids are exposed early on to disposability; of relationships, of careers, of products and services.
Of life itself.
No meaning.
No actual substance or joy.
No learning to deal with emotions and with the pain of life.
No heart. No soul.
Hopelessness.
Anger.
Abandonment by and no leadership from their parents or their institutions.
This is how we create killer kids.

killAR-15

How Our Culture Creates
Killer 15-Year-Olds

DISPOSABLE CULTURE

Disposable relationships:

Why is disposability so key to creating a savage culture and teen killers?
Simple.
Because as long as everything is disposable, temporary, then life itself ultimately becomes disposable and meaningless.
Think about it.
What do they see?
Relationships are disposable.
Marriages have long been over the fifty percent mark in failure.
People are messed up and then they marry one another.

The cycle:
And they stay messed up because they remain distracted with whatever addictions they nurture to deal with the pain of life.
Then they have kids and mess them up too because they nurture their addictions and distractions instead of their children.

Nobody gets to the heart of the matter.
Nobody goes to therapy, which likely wouldn't help anyway in today's healthcare environment because the therapists aren't getting paid by the insurance companies so they can't afford to care anyway.
Intact family units are almost completely a thing of the past.
Decimated.
Procreating is no longer part of creating a family, but often merely an unpleasant side-effect of the impulse to have sex.

Impulsive culture:

And we are impulsive.
Very impulsive.
Our culture has become like Rome in its final stages: get pleasure NOW.
Get pleasure.
Avoid pain.
Path of least resistance.
There's no making love. There's having sex. There's hooking up.
Using and abusing each other, sometimes with mutual consent, sometimes not.

Fake products and services:

Every time there is a shooting, the culture and its political leaders return to the questions of gun control and mental health.
Why does nobody talk about the corporate greed and the corporatization of government (and everything else) which takes the care out of healthcare and the substance out of products and services?
Right now there's talk of re-establishing "mental asylums" for the mentally ill---those historically cold, stark, and sometimes abusive, neglectful old institutions.
We'll debate THAT in the culture, but we won't talk about why patients get denied care at regular hospitals and at doctor's offices, even when they are paying good money for insurance---all so that CEOs of "not-for-profit" insurance companies can walk away with record profits.

The kids are lost to the profits:

No, there is no care in healthcare, including mental healthcare.
So after poorly prepared parents fail to learn how to properly parent, the healthcare system then fails to deliver proper care to these kids.
And as for other products and services, it's ALL becoming fake.
Products and services have been reduced to bottom-line profit makers---cash cows.

And nobody knows or cares to know:

Nobody actually cares either.
The people peddling the crap peddle it, and the people buying the crap buy it.
Going to the movies?
Get ready to pay a hundred bucks for your family to see that flick AFTER you watch about an hour's worth of television commercials that you could've watched for free at home!
And nobody protests this!
Just like nobody protests other crappy products and services in this devolved, overly-obvious

money grab of a culture we live
in.
We are numb to it; dumb to it.
Beaten down listless by it.

Corporatization model:

In today's business world, as soon
as   something   becomes
corporatized---in the latest, most
modern sense---there is no longer
any interest in creating substance
and excellence, only money.
That's   the   definition   of
corporatization today.

The education industry example:

Take education.
It is increasingly following the
corporate   model   just   like
healthcare.
Teachers are being forced to teach
to tests instead of to students;
and they're increasingly afraid to
be real teachers, just like
doctors are afraid to be real
doctors.
No   or   minimal   intellectual
exploration and development of the
child's intellect---just "goals"
and statistics.

What it leaves kids with:

The corporatization and anti-intellectualization of education does do one thing well: it makes for good preparation for the meaningless jobs and dead-end careers that kids will face after graduation.
Jobs and careers that do not at all nurture employees, but, instead, that just chew them up and spit them out.
Kids come out of high school barely knowing how to write or do math.

Least common denominator/robot mentality:

It's all just appealing to the least common denominator---money---as education becomes just another industry widget to be maximized on a graph; made brutally efficient by the ultimate cut---by cutting out the actual quality and the substance.
By cutting out the pursuit of excellence.

All the while teachers are having nervous breakdowns because their careers can literally depend on statistics---and learning to fake those statistics if need be for survival's sake.
That's where teachers' energies are going---survival---just like doctors' energies are going towards paperwork and billing the "right way" to accommodate a money-grabbing insurance industry that's just looking for ways not to pay them within those endless hurdles that they throw between doctor and patient.

Psychological survival over professional performance:

There is a devolution from actual professional skills and substance to energies being funneled into mere survival and survival tactics.
Nobody is striving to serve you, because they're too busy striving for survival.
That's why nobody in the service industries cares anymore. They can't care.

They're just trying to survive while the CEOs and the government power players concentrate on collecting and retaining the money and the power.

What about the kids? A distorted existence for kids:

Kids have never gotten to know life except for life in today's bottom-line profit, survival culture.
It's life and death out there.
That's all they know.
That's what we've created in them.
Sometimes literally.

Disposable careers:

What do kids have to look forward to career-wise?
Careers are disposable in this savage culture.
There's no gold watch at the end of a successful career spent striving for excellence and dedication to a field of endeavor.
In fact, there's no career, period.
Instead, organizations find a creative way to get rid of you before you can collect your full

pension benefits---or your gold watch---in other words, before you cost them or their shareholders too much off their bottom-line.
There is no loyalty.
No career development.
Nothing but bottom-line.
They'll just be slaves feeding the machine and waiting to be disposed of so that the next crop of human widgets can feed it in their turn.

Education 'smeducation:

You can be as highly educated or as highly trained as you want to be; chock full of honors, prestige, and pride in your work.
Kids today know it's all a crock.
They know---or at least have a sense---that they're just going to get chewed up and spit out by whatever corporatized entity (public or private) that hires them.

The entrepreneur's savage demise:

And if they have the courage to start their own enterprise, the vast majority of them will be chewed up and spit out by the

current, distorted version of fake
free-market capitalism, which is
not really a competition for
excellence to earn top dollar or
market share---but more a stagnant
cesspool of growing monopolies,
peddling mediocre (or worse) crap
that you HAVE to buy because it's
all the same crap being sold by
all the same, select people.
Or they'll be regulated to death
by the government, or snuffed out
by one of the aforementioned
monopolies.
And the survivors of all that will
be taken over by a bigger entity
who will turn their beloved
product or service into empty,
valueless crap---they'll use it up
as a cash cow then abandon it.

But back to getting a meaningless
job:

They take jobs where they can get
them, with minimal or no benefits
or career-development options.
No loyalty either way---not from
their employers to them, nor from
themselves to their employers.
Sometimes they work for a while,
then quit and drift for a while;

then they work for a while more, etc.
Maybe they'll "vlog" as they travel, trying to make it big that way.
And many of these are the kids with college "educations".

No real "game" in the game:

No actual, real opportunities.
No hope for their economic security or future.
And as the big players walk away with the billions, they take with them the hopes and the dreams of the generations that come after them.
They milk it for themselves and their families and friends---and they abandon us and OUR kids.
Their short-term greed robs tomorrow's potential for a strong economic and psychological infrastructure for our kids along with the real, sustainable growth of our economy; one based upon REAL, COMPETITIVE products and services---not fake products, fake careers, and get-rich quick schemes.

Stolen hope, broken promises:

They take away the hope of the
kids who would have---or
did---invest their education and
their work lives striving for
excellence on a real free-market
instead of becoming disposable
slaves making disposable widgets.
Meaninglessness.
Emptiness.
Despair.
Hopelessness.
Anger.
Rage.

USE AND ABUSE CULTURE

Addiction for everyone:

We are a culture of users.
We use each other for sex like animals without commitment or forethought.
We stay numbed up on drugs, alcohol, retail, social media, video games, working out, sports shows and apps, gambling, risky business deals, etc.
Anything to stay distracted and constantly stimulated so that we don't have to feel and we don't have to think.
Then we crash.
Addiction is a cycle and it always ends with crashing.
Addicts crash when they can't get high enough anymore to keep themselves numb from the pain of life or trauma.
Once they finally crash, there's only emptiness, pain, despair, and hopelessness.
And sometimes violence towards self and/or others.

Whenever there's a mass shooting, nobody ever asks about the addiction cycle or addiction history of the person.

Corporatized media:

The corporatized media and journalists don't even report on this at all; I know because they never ask me about it. They are corporatized, not professionals looking for truth, but bottom-line ratings and profit grabbers like every other industry in our culture.
These corporatized industries (including healthcare), are like calling a fast-food store a restaurant. Two very different agendas between a fast-food peddler and a fine dining establishment: one of profit-only, the other is product excellence THEN profit.

Back to the point:

Anyway, a recent mass shooting had as its perpetrator a man who did a lot of investing and risky business deals over his lifetime.

The media and the public remained dumbfounded for weeks about the motivation behind the shooting, searching for "clues" everywhere. Everywhere, except basic human psychology and behavior.
When a human being can no longer get high, (in this case because he'd lost lots of money recently and things were going poorly in his business ventures), hopelessness and despair set in.
It's simple addiction medicine.
And sometimes, so does violence.

Now back to the kids:

When kids, who are already weaned on the addiction cycle by their frenetic, distracted, addicted parents---and by our disposable, hedonistic culture---when those kids can no longer stay numbed up, they crash.
And sometimes violence occurs.

IDEALIZATION CULTURE

We are a culture of idealizers and we're filled with envy and entitlement.
The paths that used to eventually become available to kids from hard work and commitment are now unavailable.
Now that all careers lead to being a disposable widget and making the same; where the game is to give you as little as possible so that you still produce the crap, but you don't cost the employer anything----kids just skip the whole work hard and commit to excellence thing and simply whittle away their time strategizing on how to get instantly rich and famous.
Our strategy over substance culture; our culture where actual substance and real value and investment are NOT valued, has created a generation of pure strategists.
They see the value in strategy in our culture, and they DON'T see the value of commitment and

dedication---to anything---in our culture.

Is it cynical and lazy, or is it evolutionary adaptation?

Why toil for years in medical school or graduate school?
Why commit long-term to anything?
Kids are being raised in a culture of disposability and bottom-line profit corporatization, not one of striving for excellence to win a share of the market via honest competition.
Products and services are made to be as valueless and disposable as possible and still retain the name---and sometimes ONLY the name---of said product or service, so what do kids do?
They don't even bother with trying to spend their lives creating substance, since substance is not valued by our culture or its distorted market; only the bottom-line is valued.
Instead, they spend their lives endlessly trying (scheming?) to "break through" and "make some serious coin", with that weird, cultural, twisted sense of

entitlement and idealization of false heroes in the media and in sports and business.

No backup plan:

And when it doesn't come for the vast majority of those who aren't the lucky few; those whose combination of genetics and talents are in current demand---they crash.
There IS no backup plan.
There IS no investment in their future.
There IS no future.
And it's not a stretch for death and violence to sometimes become viable options in their young, limited minds.

IMPERSONAL ROBOT CULTURE

We've become one with our digital
devices.
We are sustained by digital
relationships from the comfort of
our bedrooms.
Aggression is easier when it's not
face to face.
People readily attack each other
through comments on social media,
without giving a thought about who
the other person is through their
digital screens.

Human devolution:

Empathy and forethought are down.
Impulsivity and disconnect are up.
We are devolving into brainstems.
And kids are coming up connected
by headphones and keyboards to
digital people through the screen.
Imagine what a kid's developing
brain must perceive as real vs.
not-real, when their entire short
lives have been so out of balance
towards the digital and the
objective and away from flesh and
blood, and the necessarily gray,

subjective, and sometimes anxiety-provoking nature of human to human relating.

Flesh and blood not real:

If flesh and blood are not registered as real in a developing kid's brain, then life and death aren't as profound either.
You can shut someone down on the internet or be aggressive verbally towards them with the touch of a keyboard or by vocal command through a headset.
Digital.
Objective.
Discrete particles, not continuous.
People become a part of your controlled world, instead of you and them a part of THE world.
YOU become the expert of your own world, like an all-powerful god.
The giver or taker of life.
Kids are given the experience that they can control their worlds entirely digitally, and that their digital worlds ARE their entire worlds.

Disconnect from reality:

There is disconnect from reality, from human suffering, from seeing someone's face when you insult them or when you reject them.
Instant aggression is readily pursued as an option, despite the fears and hesitations that would have kept it at bay and provided a balance to that impulse in the flesh and blood world.

The fatal leap:

The killer kid simply extrapolates his or her power to control his or her world to suit his or her own emotional state to also include the flesh and blood world.
Combine this with the understanding we have of the not yet fully developed, not yet fully modulated state of the adolescent brain:
Mood swings.
Impulsivity.
Lack of restraint.
Black and white thinking.
Over-generalization.
Catastrophizing.
Self-righteousness and anger.

Coupled with:

No real life experience.
No real, trustworthy relationships
(often includes unskilled
parents).
No experience on dealing with
failure, criticism, humiliation,
or rejection.
No knowledge yet of human
existential angst:
meaninglessness, mortality,
structurelessness, to name a few.

Danger:

No flesh and blood.
No humanity.
No benign guidance and leadership
from adults.
Why wouldn't we see it coming?
Flesh and blood there will indeed
be.

ANTISOCIAL AND ASOCIAL CULTURE

Antisocial means criminal minded.
Asocial means unsocial.
We always mix these terms up, but luckily, it doesn't matter right now.
Because the disconnected, unparented, increasingly impulsive and hopeless culture we live in breeds both antisocial and asocial behaviors and personalities.
And we are seeing a rise in the creation of killer kids by our culture.
See the connection?

The connection:

There is perhaps no worse direction for humans to evolve in than the combination of being more disconnected from one another on a real, flesh and blood level, combined with the increased bottom-line mentality.
Bottom-line mentality means less empathy, more goal-driven, and more pure logic driven without heart.

Ever notice how people argue on the internet?
Pure logic, no soul. No empathy. No understanding or balance. They go right for the jugular with each other.
When people are disconnected from each other, when they are only digital names on a screen or profile pictures, it becomes easier to lack empathy and to go for the jugular.
To make your point, regardless.
To focus, aim, and fire at your opponent.
This bottom-line, vicious mentality fits in perfectly well with the bottom-line, profit-above-quality mentality of our businesses and other institutions; a mentality that promotes superficial charm and superficial relationships and "networking", just like criminals pursue.
Criminals (antisocials) must USE relationships and must be superficially smart and charming to get what they want; which is to get over on you.
And THAT fits in very nicely with a culture that values strategy and

marketing and superficial appearances over actual substance, commitment, and excellence.
Money, money, money.
Power, power, power.
Gotta get mine.
NOW, add in our need for constant distraction and stimulation (alcohol, sex, working out, sports, etc.), and you have a numbed up culture that doesn't even realize that it feeds the superficial, meaningless profit machine I've just described; where nothing and NOBODY matters but the bottom-line.

The kids:

And it feeds its youth to that machine as well, and sometimes it goes very badly with that youth, like a cruel sci-fi experiment gone horribly wrong.
Now take all those factors: disconnect, emotional numbing, bottom-line antisocial behaviors and mindset, superficial relationships, meaninglessness, hopelessness, and the despair of seeing no way out of feeding the

profit machine that values nothing
and nobody.
What do you get when a young
person with the right risk
factors---both genetically and
trauma-wise (nature and
nurture)---is born into this mess
and there's no leadership to guide
him/her out of it?
No leadership at home.
No leadership in the corporatized
school system?
No leadership in the corporatized
workplace?
No leadership in government?
Only emotional incompetence and
ignorance to our own ignorance?
In the worst case scenario, you
know what you get.
Unfortunately, we all do.

SURVIVAL CULTURE

People love survival shows, zombie movies and shows, and reality shows that showcase human drama and trauma.
Why?
Because, to be blunt about it, we've become a culture of numbed up and dumbed down zombies.
Because life in our twisted, corporatized culture has become about survival, not thriving.

Joy vs. happiness:

Look around you.
Do you see joyful people around you?
Not temporarily happy, but truly joyful?
Joy is to happiness as oatmeal is to lasagna.
Joy is steady levels of happiness because you're living a life that reflects who you really are as a person. Whether in your work life or your personal relationships, your life represents the real YOU.

Happiness is like a quick fix.
Back to the addiction cycle: you get high, then you crash.
The catch phrase in our culture is "mood swing".
You can't have steady joy if you're miserable.
If your employer treats you like a slave or a widget; or like a liability to their bottom-line.
And you can't have joy if your spouse is also facing the same dehumanization and devaluation in the workplace.
All you get is miserable people being used and abused, who look for temporary relief from their constant misery by searching for "happiness".
An entire industry is built on helping you find your "happiness".
Or helping you "live as your bestest you in the whole wide world 'cause you're freaking awesome!"
Wake up.
There's no real in that.
Kids know it.
You know it.

Life is negotiation of pain:

Life is actually about pain and learning to deal with pain so you can experience joy on the other end of it.
Joy is a direct outcome of facing fears, of sacrifice, of delay of gratification, and of patience.
It's not a rocket science formula.
There's no quick fix for life.
This isn't about a drug, or a T.V. show, or a book, or a guru, or a philosophy.
People throughout time have suffered, and those who have done their best to negotiate that suffering have generally fared the best in the long run.

Adult vs. child:

It's called being an adult.
Being a real adult.
Being a competent leader of kids, not just a bigger kid.
Kids have no skills yet and no knowledge or experience yet on these matters.
So we must teach them and be models for them.
But when all they see is how we try to constantly escape pain by our addictions (addiction to

working out, drugs/alcohol, sex,
buying things, constant running
away/relocating, etc.)---that's
what they learn.
They don't learn the discipline
and the resiliency of character to
deal with the pain of life.
Because we don't have it
ourselves.
Because our culture doesn't have
it and doesn't value it.
It values the opposite.
It values mindless brainstem
zombies.
Just stay numbed up with your
addictions and your acting out;
constantly searching for and
chasing your "happiness" and your
instant fame and fortune.
Instead of forging an actual, real
life of some sort with some
commitment, some grit, and some
sort of real engagement.
No, keep running from reality and
pain and eventually you will
crash.
And, if you're lucky, you'll start
the whole empty, meaningless cycle
again.

The kids crash too:

Zombie-life is what our kids are learning from us and from our culture and that's who they're becoming because that's all they know.
And they crash too, except they're more volatile and more impulsive because they're just kids.
They have even fewer adult skills---skills like restraint, seeing the gray, and modulating anger and frustration.
If you combine the greedy, bottom-line, meaningless and empty corporatization of our money culture---which uses human beings like disposable widgets---if you combine that with our individual emotional incompetence and lack of parenting and emotional competence skills; what chance to these kids have?

SAVAGE CULTURE

If you take a moment to add up all of the above; add up everything I've discussed in the previous chapters of this book, you start to get the gist.
Take a quick look at the following list of descriptors used in this book to describe our culture:
-more impulsive
-less thoughtful
-more desperate/greater despair
-stuck/disposable careers
-used and abused
-more aggressive
-more "talking at", commenting
-less listening and learning
-more false confidence in our own expertise
-more prone to fighting/arguing
-more miserable
-more robot/zombie-like
-more disconnected
-more reactive
-less deliberate
-lacking a future
-emptiness
-meaninglessness
-more bottom-line mentality

-more greedy
-more asocial
-more antisocial
-more lies
-more fake products and services
-more strategy
-less substance
-less real
-more hopelessness
-more rage

Therein lies the problem:

The above list, which is simply a distillate of this short book, tells the whole story.
You could literally skip reading the book, and instead, you could just take this list, read it over, and ask yourself the following question:

Would I want my kid to be feeling this list of things?
Because chances are they do at least feel some of these things, or at least are thinking about them.
Why don't you go talk to your kid about it.
And, if you get a moment, take a quick second to read the appendix

chapter on parenting that
immediately follows this one
before you talk to them.
You're welcome.

APPENDIX CHAPTER: PARENTING

In some ways I've saved the best part of the book for last; I've called it the appendix.
Like so often happens in life, that which is downplayed is the most vital, the most pure; and that which is right in your face, loudly advertised and obvious, is less so.
Therefore I implore you to really read this little appendix.
Because if you read this last bit and take it to heart; if you really open yourself and your heart to it---not only will it help the kids, but, in turn, it'll help make the culture healthier as well.
That's because today's kids will flavor tomorrow's culture, just as those before us have flavored today's, both good and bad.
If we parents give kids the right stuff while they're still under our guidance and tutelage; if we help them grow strong and secure inside, then they'll feel less of what I just listed in the previous

chapter---and they'll be surrounded by less of it as well.
So work on the parenting and you'll literally change the world.
I hope this brief appendix leads you to want to learn more.

The point:

Somewhere along the line people forgot that parenting is supposed to hurt---the parent, not the child.
It's a good hurt, not a bad one.
It's the hurt of hard work and sacrifice; of patience, of longsuffering, and of a job well done.

Patience and sacrifice:

Parenting is about OUR sacrifice: of time, of physical energy, and of emotional energy.
It's about the shifting of and reorganization of our priorities---and it's often about the sacrifice of our pre-children "druthers".
And it's about patience.

Bottom-line: it's on us, not them:

Raising kids is OUR responsibility.
Not the internet's responsibility.
Not the school's responsibility.
Not their friends' responsibility.
Not even OUR friends' responsibility.
And certainly not the government's responsibility.

Your life is not YOUR life anymore:

It's pretty simple: the minute you become a parent your life is no longer YOUR life.
You now OWE somebody.
Think about it: why'd you have kids? (no offense)
Was it pride?
Was it another achievement?
Was it to keep up with others?
Was it simply an accident?
Well, whatever it was, you did it.
And they didn't ask to be born.

So you owe them:

You owe your kids.
You owe them your TIME.
You owe them your ENERGY.

You owe them your FOCUS.
You need to sacrifice some things you want.
You need to put them first.
You need to make them a priority.
Primetime, not your leftovers.
They come first now.
Not your workout.
Not sports.
Not your social life.
Not travel.
Not buying things.
Not distractions, constant "bright shiny" stimulations, or addictions.

Don't get it backwards:

YOU, the parent, must expand your skill-set and emotional competence to include them and to welcome them into this world.
You don't demand that they constrict themselves to fit your needs.
You need to do whatever it takes (therapy, reading, etc.) to grow that emotional-fat-on-the-bone so you have the excess energies and skills to give them and to lead them with.

The parenting profession:

And therein lies the problem: people become parents and try to fit their kids into their lives and into their limited capabilities too quickly, instead of trying really hard to restructure their lives (and their emotional competencies) to fit their new profession.
Yes, profession.
Parenting is a profession.
There are skills that need to be learned.
And there is your own life story and your own traumas, emotional or otherwise, to be taken care of so you don't subconsciously repeat them on your kids.
In plain English, you need to get clean from your own internal stuff so that you can be a solid leader to your kids.
Its a 24/7 profession, especially in the first ten or so years of their lives.
You are their parent, but you're also their leader, their guide, and their teacher.
You're all those things.

Pursue excellence:

And if you take it seriously and try to be excellent at it two things will occur:
Firstly, you'll heal from your own life traumas by re-experiencing parenting done right this time around, with you at the helm making it happen.
And, secondly, your kids will be healthy and strong from the inside out.
Healthier than you even.

The real, pure giving profession:

Parenting, like all true leadership, is about GIVING and SERVING.
And until you either die or have the unfortunate diagnosis of dementia, YOU REMAIN THEIR LEADER.
And if you learn to do it right, they'll always make good use of you as their leader and their guide.
Their resource and their confidant.

The question:

We lack this kind of self-sacrificing parenting in our narcissistic, morally weak culture.
And if the parents are this fragile and weak, how in the world will the kids turn out?
Well, I wrote this book to address at least one extreme answer to this question.

The solution:

Clean up the culture and clean up the parenting profession and you automatically address the phenomenon of the killer kid.

My other books, if you're interested in building up your emotional competency skills:

You, Your Marriage, Your Kids, by Anthony Ferraioli, M.D.

Don't Get Married! Unless You Understand a Few Things First, by Anthony Ferraioli, M.D.

LVAC Nation!, by Anthony Ferraioli, M.D.

Cobwebs and Ugly Wallpaper, by Anthony Ferraioli, M.D.

And if you're interested in my other books on the greed-culture:

Malignant Capitalism, by Anthony Ferraioli, M.D. and Daniel Bazile

Common-Sense Morality and the Moral-Maximum Profit Threshold, by Anthony Ferraioli, M.D.